Dance Leaders Advance

REKESHA PITTMAN

DANCE LEADERS ADVANCE

Copyright © 2013 by Rekesha Pittman.

All Scripture quotations, unless otherwise indicated, are taken from the King James Bible Version.

ISBN: 978-0-9820158-6-5

Cover Design: Kevin Vain - KDV Designs

Editors: Crystal Daniels and MarQue Woolfolk

Printed in the United States.

INTRODUCTION

Teaching about the ministry of movement over the years has been a blessing, a privilege, and a challenge. For at least the past decade, information has increased in the dance ministry realm and more dancers are seeking to study the Word of God and its stance regarding movement.

Along with the joys of teaching, I am also perplexed by the great number of those who dance both inside and outside of the church with very little information about the subject. Dance and worship conferences, workshops, seminars, online resources, training and mentoring programs, dance companies, and specialized services have multiplied by leaps and bounds. Despite the enormous pool of resources available, masses still remain undereducated about the passion so many of us proclaim.

For those who have applied the fundamental biblical studies and experienced the miraculous, we are rejoicing together. Even with the increasing information available, there is yet more for us to discover regarding this Divine opportunity to communicate the Gospel through the language of dance. Many are familiar with David and Miriam as principal dancers in the Bible. Unfortunately, for far too many the familiarity stops there. It is time to take additional steps to get a broader understanding and remove the limitations that we may have imposed upon ourselves by our own "dance ministry rulebooks."

Where the Spirit of the Lord is, there is liberty! I pray that you receive this message with an open heart, ready to receive all that the Spirit of the Lord desires to reveal through you. Let's move past the familiar and stretch beyond our own borders as true disciples of the Word in its entirety.

DEFINING A LEADER

Leadership is so much more than a title. I remember being a part of an organization several years ago and had to clarify this for one of our members. I explained to her that her designation was more of a *function* and not an exclusive title. If more leaders would **be** the designation, then the title would not come with such scrutiny!

I often tell dancers, "If you stand out front, you are a leader!" Why is this true? Even if you are not the head leader, the audience that we stand in front of views us as representatives of our local churches, organizations, and even our own countries (depending on where we travel). What we do as individuals, teams, and larger organizations can indeed open or close a door for those following us. Let's deal with the reality that we are being watched and labeled according to how we live our lives in front of others.

The King James Bible defines *leader* in several ways: In Old Testament Hebrew, the word **nagvid** (H5057) has five different meanings. Let's examine each below and see how they apply to us:

1) Captain - *Leader, especially of soldiers.* Biblically, there are many instances where we can assume a type of combat or military response to attack. We are reminded to put on the whole armor of God... Fight the good fight of faith... Instructed about our weapons of warfare, etc. In leadership, we must each know how we rank.

What do you mean, Rekesha? I am saying that we are foolish if we believe that there is no structure or rank in the movement ministry. There are "leaders of leaders" who have the training, skills, understanding and application to lead others, especially in times of conflict.

Many dance leaders face similar situations in terms of handling church politics, dealing with team members, organizing garments, managing funds, and more. Obtaining training from a Captain may help us to avert some of the conflict or minimize the damage sustained as a result of it. In the best instance, this training can also help us to become peacemakers instead of assuming a defensive stance.

If we are serving in the role of a Captain, we must understand how to properly train others in order to preserve the life of the person or ministry. There are many dancers and leaders that are crying out for direction via social media, email, and telephone calls. They are also seeking instruction through books, conferences, and online resources. Let's make sure that true Captains are disseminating the correct information that will help these soldiers survive in this field.

2) Ruler - *Leader, of a treasury.* Great leaders are good stewards over the resources that God grants. This includes people, finances, and time!

I cannot tell you the number of dance leaders who mismanage ministry funds or are ignorant of the best way to use them. It starts with us personally first! How are we managing our own finances? Are we paying our bills on time? Are we always broke? Do we have any money saved for garments, dance ministry education, and continued growth?

There is a great need for dance leaders to advance in this area! Many of us plan to attend one or more conferences each year. Some leaders travel alone, while others take entire groups. How is it that many succeed in raising the capital needed while others do not even try?

There is indeed treasure in these earthen vessels. When we put ourselves in the position to learn from other successful leaders, creativity is sparked and good management increases. Who can you glean from?

Most dance ministries today receive little to no monetary support from the local church. This is often due to lack of finances in the organization itself or a general lack of support. For some Apostles, Bishops, and Pastors, worship arts may function as a tolerable, though unnecessary activity in their opinions. This can come from a traditional background mindset or lack of passion in this area concerning that senior leader. Although we do not like to accept that this occurs, we must be aware of this if we are serving under this type of leadership.

In these cases, most movement ministries have to fund the purchase of garments, ministry education, and worship tools with personal monies or via fundraising efforts. There are many creative ways to obtain financial support, but please remember to use wisdom when requesting funds. Relationships and impact do matter!

If we expect someone to place a deposit in us, we must retain value. Just because we ask or expect someone to hand us a crisp bill does not mean that it will happen. My students often hear me say, "Look like a good investment!" Are you? Do you put careful thought into your garment selection, movement choices, and motives for ministry? Are you seeking God on a daily basis for direction? When you are a blessing, you will be blessed! I am a living witness that the Lord will move His people to give when they receive something that leaves an indelible imprint in their spirits.

With the people that you lead, are you able to be trusted? Do you do what you say, when you promised? Have you properly managed the ministry funds that have come through your hands? Let's not fool ourselves. When we are entrusted with money, we are expected to give an account for it! If the funds were raised to purchase garments, it should not "disappear" when it's time to make the transaction. Don't be tempted to borrow from something that is not yours to begin with. Temptation comes in many forms. The lack of finances presents many occasions for sin to enter in. Remain faithful over the few things so that you can rule over much!

3) Prince - *Name used for leaders of a particular tribe.* Leaders must be focused! Even Jesus was assigned to specific people during His ministry. We must know who we are appointed to for the anointing on our lives.

In the traditional understanding of the definition of prince, we know that this means the son of a king. As children of the King, we must conduct ourselves as Kingdom offspring. Is our representation as leaders primarily about ourselves, or about our Father who rules and reigns? Princes by position are under submission to the crown. Let's not take more credit than we should.

Too often, we may see someone in movement ministry do something spectacular and try to manufacture our own version of it. If it's not your area of gifting, it will not work for you over the long term! You may launch it, you may even advertise it, but if it's not your promise, it will not deliver! The same thing goes for songs and choreography. It may be their testimony, while it's only your inspiration! Abide in your calling.

Is everyone an international dance missionary? No. Don't feel pressured to step outside of your territory just because it appears like it's the popular thing to do. Obedience to God will lead you in the right path and to the right people. Many times, the Lord has said to me, "Go where you have favor." There is a difference between having favor and having fervor. Be at peace with the difference.

The Queen of England is not the monarch of the United States. We must also be aware of the limits of our influence and properly acknowledge leadership of other territories and people. The Greatest Leader was the Greatest Servant of mankind. His name is Jesus.

4) Governor - (Old Testament) *Having mastery, powerful one.* (New Testament): *To make straight, level, plain. Direct.* Leaders cannot remain amateurs if we are going to make a meaningful difference. We must be willing to obtain greater education and resources to produce a long-lasting benefit.

Government requires structure. How have we structured our ministries, businesses, relationships and legacies as leaders that will bring glory and honor to God? We cannot be deemed leaders if there is no one willing to follow us as we follow Christ.

In order to be effective at what we do, we must have the power that only comes from the endowment of the Holy Ghost! Some may rely on money and status for power, but it is the anointing that destroys the yoke! Decide to rid your life of anything that is leading you away from God or hindering your ability to lead His people righteously.

We should be able to plainly define what we are called to do and how that qualifies us for leadership. Do you have a vision and mission for your ministry, even within a church setting? Is it working or is it just pretty font on a piece of paper or filler on a website?

Dance leaders must be willing to enhance their skills and experience. Even if you have trained for many years, fresh revelation will encourage you as well as others. Even if there is no technical training near your residence, the internet, DVDs, books and personal rehearsals will assist in your improvement.

Great leaders should be able to manage people well. If you dislike people, leadership may not be a good option for you. Yes, we all have been hurt, but let's submit to God's healing so that we may govern His people appropriately.

5) Noble - *Honorable* (New Testament) **hodegeo** (G3594) *To be a guide, lead on one's way, to guide. To be a guide or a teacher. To give guidance to.* We should not do anything that would inhibit the honor on our lives and ministries. When we live lifestyles that are contrary to God's Word, we produce dishonor. In order for us to serve as guides that are reliable, we have to be diligent examples.

Are we encouraging those who follow us to gossip, complain, compete, or show a lack of respect for others who are serving the Gospel cause? Beyond the rivalries that exist in movement ministries, many dancers openly disrespect Pastoral leaders, ministry directors, and core biblical mandates. Let us continue to lead through our actions and not solely through our words.

TYPES OF DANCE LEADERS

Do you know that you are not the first of your kind? Many would argue over who is the founder of "liturgical dance" in their respective countries, but as intrinsic as dance is in the fabric of many cultures, it's hard to tell. As the first dancer mentioned in the Scriptures, I am sure that Miriam would have a hearty discussion with us about who blazed the path first!

The bottom line is that there are many who have gone before us and many more who will come after us and we can learn from them all. We should indeed know those who labor among us!

It is surprising to me to survey many up-and-coming dance leaders who know very little about the existing leadership already active in movement ministry. It is not for a lack of availability of information. This is simply ignorance and a refusal to investigate.

I have met several prominent leaders in dance ministry, but I knew who they were before we ever said, "Hello," or exchanged glances. I would visit every internet search engine in existence and look for "Praise Dance," "Worship Dance," "Liturgical Dance," and other terms that would come to mind. As a result, I discovered a vast pool of wonderful co-laborers who shared my passion and enthusiasm. When we are properly prepared, we will avoid the embarrassment of becoming too common with people that we should show honor and respect.

There are several types of "leadership levels" that we should be aware of as it pertains to the ministry of movement. Let's truly challenge ourselves to be well-versed in our area of service. Giving honor to whom honor is due is a must!

Local Dance Leaders

A Local Dance Leader serves in a local church. Usually, all of the ministry members belong to the same congregation and submit under one leader or ministry director. This level of leadership often encounters the challenges of dealing with church politics in the areas of frequency of activity, attire, song selection, finances, and accepting outside invitations. Many times, leaders in this area have minimal experience in dance training or managing people.

Local Dance Leaders experience pressure from leadership, the congregation, other dancers, parents of children and teens, and maintaining a personal life. We must continue to pray for the many local leaders that struggle, become wounded, and refuse to pursue greater understanding in the worship arts.

Community Dance Leaders

A Community Dance Leader can serve people from various churches, surrounding cities, denominations, and cultural backgrounds. These visionaries may run a community dance troupe, dance company, or performance group. Their influence may extend throughout the city or region where they serve.

One of the many challenges of serving as a Community Dance Leader is that they may have to deal with people who have different doctrinal backgrounds, cultural traditions, or core beliefs. Even though many people profess to be "Christian," how that is defined as a lifestyle differs greatly for many people. This is when basic standards must be applied that govern all members of a community dance organization. It may be wise to avoid disputes concerning church practices, require salvation through Jesus Christ, discuss appropriate conduct for a minister of the Gospel through movement, and define membership expectations.

It is also a good practice to have an accountability system in place. Community Dance Leaders must remain sensitive to the requirements that dancers have within their own church homes and the expectations of their own church leadership. It would be wise not to get into a spiritual "tug-of-war" concerning conflicting dates, but rather take the time to prepare for them.

In order for most Community Dance Leaders to have a following, at least some level of skill is required in the area of movement, teaching, or choreography. Though the load can be shared with other team leaders in these areas, the expectation is that the leader has a firm understanding of how to do them all so that the unit does not collapse if another leader or member decides to leave the group.

National Dance Leaders

National Dance Leaders have influence in several areas of their nation or country. This may represent many cultures, traditions, and church denominations. This requires a great level of reliance on the Holy Spirit, a skilled application of biblical teaching, and a track record of success.

On the national dance platform, there must be a discernment of the greater issues that the worship in dance community endures in the realm of shared experience as well as practical application of movement ministry concepts. This leader often travels to different States, cities, townships, communities, and peoples, providing technical training, educational instruction, and resource recommendations.

The National Dance Leader frequently serves as a mentor, adviser and counselor to other local, community, and national dance leaders. This can take place in person, via electronic communication, on the phone, during a teleconference, and through social media networks. A growing sector of national dance leaders are becoming authors, bloggers, and social media activists for the worship arts community.

Also growing among many National Dance Leaders is a greater function in the Body as Apostles, Pastors, Elders, Prophets and other offices in the larger church community. This is not merely limited to the teaching of movement, but a general calling to serve as a minister of the Gospel.

Most often, the National Dance Leader is skilled in both movement and teaching. Even more creatively, some of these leaders are becoming entrepreneurs in the area of garment creation, authorship, workshops, educational materials, and internet commerce.

As a National Dance Leader, a life committed to prayer and Bible study will help to avert the temptation to be "served" more than being a servant. Frequent compliments, monetary donations, platforms, verbal acknowledgments, and other accolades can lead to pride and an eventual downfall if not carefully guarded against.

International Dance Leaders

"Go ye therefore" is the mandate for the International Dance Leader. Usually a trailblazer of sorts, this leader is innovative, impactful, and experienced. Blessed with the grace to minister to many cultures, this leader must maintain a dedicated prayer life and submission to the Holy Spirit for movement, guidance, decision-making, and protection.

Depending on popularity, this leader may have a whirlwind schedule for several weekends throughout the year, especially during "Dance Conference Season" (the summer). Depending on the area of residence, this leader often travels by airplane or car, and endures long hours on the road in addition to the requirements of being prepared to teach, preach, or choreograph.

Because a high level of responsibility rests on the shoulders of the International Dance Leader, this "Leader of Leaders" may have an administrative staff, businesses, a finance team, and a dance team in addition to responsibilities at the local church, to the family, and a need to take care of themselves! For the truly called, this is not glamorous work. Balance must be planned in advance, or it can be easy for this level of leader to become overwhelmed.

The International Dance Leader is often highly skilled in movement, teaching, and preaching, and often has a prophetic gift. This leader is sought out by many cultures as an authority on a global level, whose application of foundational teaching and administration speaks across language barriers and racial lines. This distinct leader is usually highly-respected, and has peer relationships with other International Dance Leaders as well as with Apostles, Bishops, Pastors, politicians, and other influential leaders.

International Dance Leaders may be published authors, network leaders, entrepreneurs, and influencers on a large scale. Frequently, these leaders have been ordained as Apostles, Pastors, Reverends, Elders, Deacons, Ministers and other designations as the church deems appropriate.

Without a passport, the international leader cannot truly go into all nations. There is no need to wait for an invitation to obtain one. If you have been called to the nations, move in obedience today!

First, Giving Honor

I repeat: We must know them that labor among us! Many of us dishonor those who have gone before us by remaining ignorant to what is taking place in the larger liturgical dance community. I am blessed to teach leadership at many dance conferences and am baffled by the lack of awareness of dance leaders regarding the Scriptures and other leaders in this field

POP QUIZ

How many dance leaders can you name from each of the categories previously outlined?

Do your research online if you must!

Local:

_____

_____

Community:

_____

_____

16

National:

_____

_____

International:

_____

_____

Comparative Biblical Studies
of Dance Leaders

In accordance with the categories outlined, let's take a look at a few examples of biblical dance leadership:

JEPTHAH'S DAUGHTER: LOCAL

And Jephthah came to Mizpeh unto his house, and, behold, his daughter came out to meet him with timbrels and with dances: and she was his only child; beside her he had neither son nor daughter.
- Judges 11:34 (KJV)

As a "local" leader, Jephthah's daughter did not have "a name" per se. She is defined by her father, which in many cases for local dance leaders is a Pastor or church organization. Jephthah's daughter demonstrated loyalty through obedience. Her relationship with

17

her father prompted her to dance upon his return. She was also aware of the practiced tradition of the closest female relative to greet the returning victor with timbrels and dances. She sacrificed her own life aspirations to submit to the vow made by her father. (See Judges Chapter 11 in its entirety for more in-depth study)

In comparing the Local Dance Leader with Jephthah's daughter, his or her identity can be hidden behind another leader, organization, or denomination. Often this position can be based on relationship. Local leaders can be greatly challenged concerning the area of position because their leadership is often based on a designated title alone, at least in the beginning. If leadership is not developed on the local level, this leader may be frustrated by resistance, lack of influence with higher-level leadership, and feeling that their own desires, visions, and creativity is being stifled by the expectations of higher leadership.

MIRIAM: NATIONAL

And Miriam the prophetess, the sister of Aaron, took a timbrel in her hand; and all the women went out after her with timbrels and with dances.
- Exodus 15:20 (KJV)

Miriam had the capacity to lead all of the women of the children of Israel in dances. As a prophetess, she was a voice to her nation and influenced many tribes. In a position of high visibility, she had access to high-ranking leadership (Moses), and was very outspoken.

One of Miriam's downfalls was that she was prideful and got to the point where she felt that she could openly challenge God-ordained authority.

National Dance Leaders have to be careful to understand his or her realm of influence, and still be able to humbly submit to governing powers. The classification of celebrity can cause a leader that once served as a watchman to claim equal status to leaders that the Lord may have placed above them. Miriam was older than Moses, so this was not an issue of age, but of function.

Because many National Dance Leaders have the privilege to travel to many areas, they must be careful to submit to spiritual rank and order in other territories out of respect to the Lord's governing structure. Seniority in age or years of service does not grant the National Dance Leader a license to usurp authority. A careful resolve to remain submitted to the Holy Spirit will quench any presumptuous (and ultimately, rebellious) tendencies that this level of service may produce.

DAVID: INTERNATIONAL

"Then David danced before the LORD with all his might; and David was wearing a linen ephod. So David and all the house of Israel brought up the ark of the LORD with shouting and with the sound of the trumpet."
- 2 Samuel 6:14-15 (NKJV)

King David governed his kingdom and influenced those around him. Even before King David was recorded dancing like a madman in the Scriptures, his very legacy provoked women to dance in his honor, even in the presence of their current king, Saul! His influence was large-scale:

> *"Now it had happened as they were coming home, when David was returning from the slaughter of the Philistine, that the women had come out of all the cities of Israel, singing and dancing, to meet King Saul, with tambourines, with joy, and with musical instruments. So the women sang as they danced, and said: "Saul has slain his thousands, and David his ten thousands." Then Saul was very angry, and the saying displeased him; and he said, "They have ascribed to David ten thousands, and to me they have ascribed only thousands. Now what more can he have but the kingdom?" So Saul eyed David from that day forward."*
> - 1 Samuel 18: 6-9 (NKJV)

It must be uncomfortable to be openly celebrated at someone else's party! Notice that it said that the women came out to meet King Saul, not King David! Imagine the sheer numbers of women dancing in the streets if entire cities came out to make this declaration. It must have been difficult for Saul to accept that he would be replaced by an emerging leader...

It is not a coincidence that International Dance Leaders face many of these same challenges. Some of these leaders may travel more frequently than their local church leadership, and may even have a larger influence in terms of worldwide reach. David's influence became a cause for contention and envy from his leader. This does not need to happen if all leaders continue to submit to the Lord! Instead of becoming envious, leaders who lead leaders can open the door for mentoring, guidance, and direction.

Current leadership should not get nervous when other leaders of influence arise. This is the natural course of succession. If International Dance Leaders allow ministry titles and designations to make self-preservation a greater motive than the advancement of the Gospel to God's glory, all manner of competition, strife, division, and mayhem will result!

As David grew as a King and international leader, his influence continues to impact us today. I regularly ask dancers, "Who danced in the Bible?" The number one name mentioned is David. I am sad to say that this is the extent of the biblical knowledge of still too many in the dance ministry.

David was anointed, spent time with God, understood music, experienced a wide range of emotions, worshipped publicly and privately, and led others in worship. Often, people use David as a shining example of God's favor concerning the man who was after His heart. Let's not forget: David was not able to build the dream house that he planned for God because he had blood on his hands. Leaders must keep their hands pure in order to see dreams and visions come to pass unhindered. Leaders must confront and deal with character flaws that will prove a hindrance and not a help.

HERODIAS' DAUGHTER: CORRUPT LEADERSHIP

Then an opportune day came when Herod on his birthday gave a feast for his nobles, the high officers, and the chiefmen of Galilee. And when Herodias' daughter herself came in and danced, and pleased Herod and those who sat with him, the king said to the girl, "Ask me whatever you want, and I will give it to you." He also swore to her, "Whatever you ask me, I will give you, up to half my kingdom." So she went out and said to her mother, "What shall I ask?" And she said, "The head of John the Baptist!" Immediately she came in with haste to the king and asked, saying, "I want you to give me at once the head of John the Baptist on a platter." And the king was exceedingly sorry; yet, because of the oaths and because of those who sat with him, he did not want to refuse her.
- Mark 6:21-26 (NKJV)

It's hard for us to discuss, yet it is the truth: There is corruption in our ranks! While many of us are pro-moting and celebrating unity in the dance community, there are some leaders who have ulterior motives. Believe not every spirit! This is less a cause for alarm and more so a call for discernment. We must be careful not to form allegiances with spiritual wolves, corrupt operators, and self-absorbed egotists. There is too much at stake!

Herodias' daughter was very powerful. She was a master-performer who knew how to get what she wanted by using what she had. She used her influence to gain access to leadership, but behind the scenes was a puppet master with a sinister agenda! Herodias' daughter was a people-pleaser who enjoyed the attention of the crowd. This is not the type of dance leader that any of us should aspire to become.

Here is a Prophetic warning that was revealed to me by God in December of 2012:

"HERODIAS' DAUGHTER is being platformed for a season. Beloved, all opportunities for exposure are not from God. This spirit wants to silence the voice of the prophetic that would bring correction to error in leadership, position, and authority. Seductively pleasing onlookers, this opportunist obtains favor and then makes diabolical requests. Instead of setting captives free, it seeks to destroy them. Do not be dazzled by appearances, excellent speech or talents. These can all be coached... Let's tune in to the voice of the Lord concerning EVERY connection that we make, and adjust accordingly."

We must pray for the Lord to cleanse us completely from impure motives, hidden agendas, a desire for attention, and the need to be rewarded by people for our participation. As we have a commission to preach the Gospel, we cannot allow money, power, position, or authority to compromise our obedience to God. Let's all be the type of leader who gets the following stamp of approval from the Lord: WELL DONE!

Characteristics of a Good Dance Leader

Not everyone who dons ballet shoes is handpicked by God! Because dance ministries have become as common in many churches as the ever-popular praise teams, some Pastors and leaders may ask people who are largely unqualified to serve in an area that is not even a passion or a priority. This can cause more harm than good. As a basic foundation for dance leaders, here are some attributes that will be helpful for effective leadership:

1) An intimate relationship with God

2) A strong, consistent prayer life

3) Regular church attendance and biblical study

4) Submission to leadership

5) A teachable spirit

6) A servant's heart

7) A desire for education (spiritual and movement vocabulary)

8) A genuine love for people

9) Patience, patience, and more patience!

10) Creativity
11) Sensitivity to the Holy Spirit
12) The ability to lead themselves, and then others

This list is not all-inclusive, but outlines some basic principles needed for endurance in ministry.

Many spiritual attacks arise in the arts. Without proper understanding, much heartache, tears, and re-bellion will manifest in the movement ministry. The more education that dance leaders pursue in the area of Bible study, concentrated worship arts studies, and attendance of Godly gatherings will help to divert some of the common pitfalls that plague dance ministries.

RESOURCES FOR LEADERS

In this time of technological advancements, we have almost unlimited access to dance ministry resources. As dance leaders, we must insist on investing in our ministries. Time, money, and training are needed in order to advance beyond the ordinary. I am not saying that we must pay our way into leadership, but valuable items, information, and education often come with a price.

Dance Ministry Books

Name at least four dance ministry books that have been written, along with the names of the authors: (You can research them online if you are unsure)

1)

_____

2)

_____

3)

_____

4)

_____

Dance Conferences and Workshops

The list of conferences, conventions, and workshops in movement ministry continues to grow exponentially. Although arts education is encouraged, we will not be able to distinguish fact from fable if we ourselves do not become accurate students of the Word of God. The danger of veering away from the Word as it pertains to our ministries is that we can morph dance ministry into "the traditions of men" if we embrace our personal preferences over accurate biblical teaching.

What major dance ministry events are held regularly that you have attended or would like to support (Internationally, Nationally, and Locally)?

Write at least three hosted events below:

1)

_____

2)

_____

3)

_____

Are there any workshops near your geographic location that you can support? YES / NO

Are there any online dance ministry trainings or programs that you are considering? YES / NO

With appropriate planning, conference attendance does not have to cause financial strain. Look ahead and see what the Lord is prompting you to attend. We have done several creative fundraisers to assist with travel expenses. Often, airfare can be the most expensive, then hotel, then registration—please don't forget about food! Tackle the most expensive items first, remembering to take advantage of any early bird savings that many conferences offer for supporting in advance.

Dance Classes

Training will not drain your anointing! Do not be fearful of challenging yourself to grow in your movement vocabulary. Research some classes available in your area that may benefit you. If there are no in-person classes available, this may be an area of need that you can meet after mastering at least the basics.

While the demand for Christian-based movement instruction is growing, we can still glean from traditional dance classes. Let's make sure to let our lights shine even in these instances! I took African Dance classes for a season and enjoyed them; however, if there were dances that seemed a bit too seductive or dealt with an "unholy" spirit, I declined to participate by remaining standing or moving toward the rear of the class. Instead of African attire, I wore a praise dance overlay. The class knew that I was a "praise dancer" and embraced me.

If you cannot obtain training personally, there are instructional videos available for purchase or obtainable online. Make sure to challenge yourself without injuring yourself! If you run a dance team or group dance ministry and you cannot afford to take classes individually, a more experienced dancer may be the trainer that you are looking for! Don't be afraid to bring the dance class to your location.

Online Dance Ministry Resources

There are blogs, resource websites, video trainings, teleconferences, and emerging apps out there! Why wait for something "magical" to appear in front of you? Get in front of a computer, go to a search engine and see what you can find!

Garment Resources

There are commercial garment manufacturers, ministry designers, seamstresses, tailors, oh my! Don't be confined to what "everyone else is wearing," but please remember that immodesty leads to closed doors! Many amazing dance ministry garment suppliers can be found at dance conferences, online, or even in your local assembly through a seamstress or tailor! PRAY first, and then conduct your research.

Never base your garments on how "cheap" you can find them. I have many garments that look very expensive but the truth is that the Lord has given me favor, blessed me with garments, and allowed me to find good deals. Other times, I invested in more expensive pieces that still look as good as they did the day that I purchased them several years ago.

Yes, it does matter what we wear and the Bible is full of descriptive, colorful and meaningful attire. When we seek the Lord first, His design will never leave us inadequately covered. If you see someone wearing a garment that speaks to you, ask them where they got it from. Dance leaders must take responsibility for proper covering.

Dance Ministry Tip: For my dance company, we have a "Keeper of the Wardrobe." Don't worry, it's biblical:

> *"So Hilkiah the priest, and Ahikam, and Achbor, and Shaphan, and Asahiah, went unto Huldah the prophetess, the wife of Shallum the son of Tikvah, the son of Harhas, **keeper of the wardrobe**; (now she dwelt in Jerusalem in the college;) and they communed with her."*
>
> - 2 Kings 22:14 (KJV)

This leader takes our measurements, orders garments, delivers garments, and keeps inventory for the dance company. She also researches our garment options for the future.

As a leader, I have a passion for garments, but I do not have the time (or the trunk space) to carry garments for a large group of dancers. Inquire if there is someone (a dancer or supporter) that is willing and able to manage this important responsibility.

Purposefully Speaking

Each movement ministry should serve a distinct purpose! If you are a church-based dance ministry, your purpose should line up with the vision for your church. Many misunderstandings evolve from improper expectations of both the dancers and church leaders. If you cannot submit to the directives and decisions made in your local assembly, maybe that dance leader position is not for you.

After embracing the purpose of your church, understand in what context the movement ministry serves the purpose of that church. As a ministry, you can have a separate vision and mission statement that aligns with the one that has already been decreed. Establishing and maintaining a ministry vision serves as a checkpoint to make sure that we have not strayed away from our assignment.

Community, National and International dance ministries should also have clear vision. Encourage each participant to memorize and be able to recite and write the vision in its entirety. If properly encouraged, this will aid in minimizing confusion, guide decision-making, and maintain order. Whether it is for a soloist, duet, group, company, or international network, applied vision is necessary for advancement. Having words written on paper or a website that we do not embody is useless. Let's live the vision that God gives.

When writing your vision/mission statement, consider the following questions and write your responses below:

1) What does your ministry do?

_____

2) Who is your ministry for?

_____

3) Who will your ministry reach?

_____

Be careful not to copy the vision that the Lord already gave to someone else! We cannot advance if we refuse to seek the Lord for ourselves. I remember seeing the vision and mission that the Lord gave me for Reign Dance Company on another website, verbatim, with only the name of our group changed. I was floored! Again, I cannot stress enough the importance of seeking God first. We perish without the vision.

AREAS OF ADVANCEMENT

With the increasing availability of information, the dance and movement ministries are growing by leaps and bounds! There are several areas that we can consider in terms of advancement or moving forward. These are a few of the growing industries that are being impacted by the arts. This list will continue to lengthen as revelation increases.

Education

Dance ministry is finding its way into the educational system via several avenues. Many prominent dance ministry leaders have launched training institutes and online educational opportunities for enrollment. Some are accredited and others are not, but these offerings have increased an appetite for learning in the dance ministry community.

Movement ministry is gaining a foothold in the traditional educational system as well. Not only is this information becoming widespread in seminaries, but through traditional arts studies also. As college students enroll as dance majors as undergraduates, master's level students and through the completion of doctoral studies programs, colleges and universities are expanding the arts curriculum to consider this "cultural" form of dance.

For those who have not yet decided to go the route of formal education, many more are purchasing and publishing books on this subject. As dance ministry is largely a niche or specialty market, many dance leaders are self-publishing literary works as informational and instructional tools. One challenge with self-publishing is that there are less systems in place to ensure that the information being shared is accurate.

Traditional publishing houses have editors, marketing plans and distribution agreements that are largely out of reach to self-publishers due to the expense involved. This should not deter a dance leader from publishing. When the Lord instructs someone to release a Word, obedience is the only option!

Obtaining books on the subject of dance ministry is relatively easy through Amazon. In addition to paperback books for purchase, you may also download books for reading on your tablet, telephone or computer through the use of apps. Technology is making our barriers disappear! There are some great books and information out there. Always remember to research everything that you read for yourself.

Technical Development

I currently laugh at the notion, but when I first started out in dance ministry, I thought that taking formal dance classes would somehow compromise the anointing that I had to dance without it! It seems silly to me now, but eventually I realized that it was only fear of feeling inadequate that was holding me back.

Enrolling in my first dance class as an adult was a challenging process, but the rewards outweighed my doubts. Depending on where you live, you may be able to take in-person classes at a community college, local dance studio, arts development program, or even a local church. If there are no obvious classes in your area, don't give up. There may be someone residing near you who is willing to come to your location to teach technical instruction. There is always the option of taking classes via DVD or online, but adopting great form may be limited without correction or feedback from an instructor. As it has often been said, "Where there's a will, there's a way!"

If you are able to find in-person classes, be sure to be consistent in your attendance. Advancing in technique will take many hours of training for those who are not naturally built for dance. Do not be afraid to try different styles of dance training, although you may not want to take them all at once! Be sure to invest in quality dance shoes and make time to stretch as often as you can.

In order for movement ministry to be taken seriously outside of the parameters of our church facilities, we must be able to communicate in a language that is widely understood. Skill-enhancement will only propel us forward. Embrace the challenge to advance in dance technique, whatever your level of experience.

Personal Care

As dance and movement leaders, we must remember to take care of ourselves. If we are not careful, it may become easy to neglect proper eating habits, personal care, and managing our time properly. For most professional dancers, body maintenance is a requirement. Although this standard is not widely enforced for dance ministry, we must be realistic about our ability to be used in terms of stamina and longevity.

I have struggled with my weight for as long as I can remember. Although I maintain a high standard of discipline in most areas of my life, I have an appetite for sweet, salty, and fatty! I have conquered obesity before, but after having my first child, this challenge became harder than ever!

There was a distinct time that I can remember ministering on a program with all of my might. As I returned to my seat, I had a dizzying sensation. Suddenly, it sounded like someone turned the volume in my ears all the way down, and the room began to get dark. I was beginning to faint! I immediately knew that this was a result of my excess weight and began to make changes. This included adopting an exercise regime and embracing healthy eating habits.

Don't put your trust in the latest diet craze. I laugh now when I think about times when I thought that I could eat low-fat and fat-free foods until I was stuffed, without understanding the high caloric content present in many of these foods. Dancers should have a general awareness and understanding of fat, calories, protein, fiber and serving sizes if we are to understand the type of fuel that we are putting into our bodies. It may take us some time to break bad habits, but with practice, we will prevail!

Neglecting our bodies can hinder us as dance leaders. Dry and cracked feet, broken fingernails, parched skin and unkempt hair may have others questioning our good judgment… While many of us are doing good deeds by taking care of others, we will eventually become sidelined when we run out of steam.

You may be asking yourself how physical appearance has anything to do with this? What is showing on the outside generally reflects what is happening inside of us physically, mentally and spiritually. We do not have to have a big budget in place to maintain ourselves. Pay someone if you must, but making time and securing the proper tools to care for ourselves will serve just fine.

As far as your health is concerned, please visit a doctor at least once per year for a routine exam. Resist the urge to neglect any physical warning signs before it is too late. Even if you are unable to afford health-care, make plans to have some type of assessment completed so that your health is not compromised.

Many dance leaders have a habit of running from sun-up to sundown with rehearsals, engagements, and a long list of personal responsibilities. Ensure that you get sufficient rest in the form of sleep and relaxation before your body decides to make the choice for you! Falling asleep at the wheel or being inattentive in a worship service due to extreme exhaustion will not end well. Additionally, lack of energy can result in injury. The Lord gave us an example of resting as a necessity. Let's follow His lead.

Outreach

If we only serve our own needs, we are not fulfilling the Great Commission. Since the word "minister" means *to serve*, dance leaders must be servants that train other servants. Developing our teams to positively impact our surroundings will enhance our sensitivity, understanding and connection to others.

We can reach our local communities through service. This can either be through the arts or through meeting the needs of others. Our dance company serves our local community by offering free work-shops on the basics for ministries that are starting or need adjustments. Another idea is to sponsor another ministry by providing garments, worship instruments, or books as a show of solidarity and unity. There are many opportunities to feed the homeless, read books to children, visit hospitals and nursing homes, and show love to others. Whatever you do, stretch beyond your comfort zone!

There may also be invitations for mission trips through movement. There are many missionaries and mission groups going into the world to spread the Gospel. Not only can we support the mission trips of others, we must also be prepared to go beyond our borders if God is calling us to serve in the mission fields.

My first trip to South Africa allowed me to discover my calling as a Worship Arts Missionary. Not only did the Lord send a prophet to tell us that we would be going to South Africa specifically, four short months later, the Lord provided all of the funds needed for a team of us to go! We prepared clothing, diapers and finances for food distribution as traditional missionaries provide, but the Lord had another revelation planned...

One of the South African Pastors told me that, while feeding his people for one day was fine, it was better to think about how to sustain a community over a period of time. I then realized that our efforts would only be a temporary fix, though well-intentioned. As we continued to provide arts workshops for dancers, singers and musicians in various townships, I handed out several books as a gift. To see other artists clutching my books to their chests like they were prized possessions touched my heart. After we would finish dancing, our newfound friends would inquire if they could have the CD of the music or ask where they could get it. We ended up giving them away.

I felt so underprepared! How could I teach dancers about proper ministry attire if they had no access to it? Why was I waving flags and raising billows and just leaving it up to them to figure out how to continue this wonderful mode of expression being demonstrated? I then resolved to make a difference for every future mission that the Lord would bless me to undertake. As

I continue to travel to the nations, I include a request for funds to provide books, garments, flags, billows and music as part of my seed to "sow" into that land. Equipping His saints for His work will leave a deposit that will last beyond my short time with them. Our God is awesome!

Relationship Development

If we are truly Kingdom-minded, we realize that we need other parts of our body in order to function completely. As dance leaders, we cannot allow ourselves to become content with adopting the "lone ranger" syndrome by thinking that we are able to solve everything on our own. Make efforts to connect with other leaders and spiritual counsel as often as you can. Valuing these relationships will remind you that you are not alone in this.

Technology

We would be foolish to ignore the fact that people are attached to technology more than ever. There is now instant access to videos, pictures, and immediate feedback more than ever. If you have been to a dance concert or conference lately, you can instantly view images and dances via social media because of uploading. As a result, it is very difficult to control what appears online about our ministries and personal lives. Let's continue to put our best foot forward at all times.

We must make a decision concerning how we want to represent our relationship with God when it comes to social media. Over the years, I have had to adjust what I say, limit pictures that I post, and consider my comments to others. I realize that many people are looking for me to provide an example of consistency during my virtual "public appearances." If I quote Scripture in one post and then rant and rave in anger on the next, I am limiting my ability to lead on a large scale.

Consider your own pictures, posts, videos and responsive commentary. Would Jesus be proud to claim you as a friend or follower? As an author, I am always aware of my grammar, spelling and word choices. Why would anyone want to purchase my books if I appear to be illiterate? Why should someone support your ministry or group if they see pictures of you sitting at a bar on Saturday, yet praising Him in church on Sunday? Please be mindful that while some things are not "sins" in themselves, we should not do, say, or show something that would cause others to stumble.

When it comes to websites, there are several options from which to select. You can pay a small yearly fee to secure your own custom domain. There are also service providers who allow you to build a website that retains a portion of their own domain name. Whichever medium you choose, understand that your choice is communicating with your visitors. "Free" websites make it more challenging to give ministries serious financial backing. Why should others invest more than you are willing to do for yourself? At whatever level you can, excel!

If you have a website, the domain name should reveal its intended purpose. It may not be a good idea to sell intimates and promote your ministry on the same website! If you are serious about this ministry, make the best investment that you can for great results. Many webhosts offer great do-it-yourself site-building software. Don't think that you have to spend thousands of dollars to get online. At the very least, your website should contain information about your ministry, how to contact you, and any other pertinent information. Visit other great ministry websites for information (but not necessarily for imitation!).

One great and inexpensive way to communicate with an audience is through an online blog. A blog is used to express opinions, share news, promote events, and have interactive discussions. Most people can start a free blog or pay a small monthly fee for more flexibility and customization. Explore your options!

Anyone with a cell phone, tablet, or computer has heard about the vast availability of apps available for download. I often use GPS for directions to ministry events for places that I am visiting for the first time. My apps also allow me to blog, post comments or upload pictures onto social media sites. If you are not carrying a printed Bible, there is an app for that! As an example, my dance company records our rehearsals on a cell phone and we upload it to our private group Facebook page for review and practice on our own time. We have found this to be very helpful, not only for personal implementation, but for documentation of our dances.

Finances

Every dance leader who is passionate about this ministry understands the great financial investment that comes with leading in this area. I cannot tell you the number of garments that I have purchased, not only for myself, but for entire ministries! Not only that, but going to conferences and workshops meant that I had to have the latest book, flag or resource for dance ministry. Yes, that was what I did in the beginning... Whew!

Eventually, I had to figure out a way to budget. It makes no sense to pay large sums of money for events, garments, and worship instruments and return home broke. I had to learn to plan for my travels in advance, and fundraise or save money to invest in the ministry. Now, I teach these same principals to my teams. Who wants to go to a conference and be unable to afford to eat? We must count the cost before going out to the big dance.

As dance leaders, we must not be content with looking good only in our garments and during routines. Are there bill collectors calling you? Are you drowning in debt? Do others have difficulty reaching you by phone because you are "temporarily unavailable?"

Are you neglecting any of your primary fiscal responsibilities by making impulse purchases on material, dance attire, and by giving offerings that you cannot afford? We must all yield to the Holy Spirit in these matters and know that when He leads us, it will result in a return on investment. Make the necessary adjustments so that you are able to get education and equipment without being evicted.

Fundraising

Speaking of finances, some dance ministries have no idea where to begin when it comes to fundraising. Having a 501c3 status does not guarantee large grants and cash flow. Strategic planning, wisdom, and building a solid reputation will help us succeed in our fundraising efforts.

My first word of advice to anyone expecting people to give is to be excellent. Excellence commands a response in some way. For the first dance conference that I'd ever hosted, a lady walked up to us during the event and handed us $500.00! There have been many times since then that people have walked up to me and placed significant amounts of money in my hands after ministry. There was no call for an offering, just a mandate to give the Lord my very best.

Maintaining this standard, we have also received telephone calls to dance at events that include an honorarium or love offering of some sort. This can range from a few dollars to several hundred dollars for a local event. While I do not personally charge an amount for ministry, the Lord has moved on the hearts of His people to bless us bountifully!

The opportunities for fundraising for people of excellence are limitless! Do not restrict what the Lord can do in your life. For my first international mission trip, I watched God work miracles. My team and I received a prophecy during a worship service that we would be going to South Africa. "Great," I thought, "One day we will get to go!"

Little did I know, that day would come sooner than I could have imagined. Three weeks later, I was teaching at a conference out of State. At the end of the evening, a gentleman approached me and told me that he was a South African Minister. He said, "We would like for you and your team to come to South Africa!" I was amazed because I did not bring my team along with me for that trip.

Within a few weeks, we had a date for our mission! When we got an estimate for the cost, it was over three thousand dollars! How in the world could we raise that amount of money in just a few months? A short while later, I saw someone asking for money for a mission trip to South Africa via social media. I immediately sent her a donation.

We designed a flyer and began asking for support. We set up a PayPal button, sent out emails, wrote letters, and told our churches that we were going overseas. We prayed, we danced, we baked goodies, we asked for money. We kept one another encouraged. Online donations, cash and checks came pouring in! We even set up a "blessing basket" at rehearsal for people to give to those who were raising funds. At the end of the week, we would donate whatever amount was in there to one of the members of the mission team. Some of us raised so much money that we were able to "overflow" into the efforts of another team member. At the end of three months, seven of us boarded a plane on South African Airways! God is able!

We raise funds for retreats, travel, fabric, tools and other needs in several ways. We have sold tickets to productions, hosted dance concerts, organized dinner banquets, promoted community choreography classes for a small donation, sold catalog items and cookies, and directly asked for financial support. With God's favor, we have been able to succeed in our efforts. Pray about a formula or a combination of creative efforts that will work for you. Be sure to get permission to do so from your leadership, and make sure that you use the money for the purposes that they were raised.

If you are undertaking a massive assignment, there are innovative ideas out there for fundraising. You may apply for grants, secure investors, or discover the growing trend of "crowd funding" to finance your efforts. This is an account that is set up online for anyone to invest in, that provides incentives for the level of investment made. Crowd funding is being used to make independent films, finance book publishing, develop software, and more! Want to build or open a dance studio? Research your options. No limits!

Product Development

One way to earn an income in ministry is through a product line. If you are merely into making money, you may not make much of it because people tend to discern greed over time. You do not have to replicate what you see another dance leader or marketplace minister doing. If garments are not your skill, please leave them to those who have the ability to produce them with quality.

There may be a book inside of you. You may want to produce a video. You may make flags, banners or streamers. Yet, these are not the only options in movement ministry. Tapping into Divine creativity through prayer, Bible study and worship will cause a Holy Spirit download to overtake you. There is nothing new under the sun, but we are still discovering things that have been hidden from us for generations.

I have been able to generate income through writing and publishing books on dance and movement ministry. Even though I have a degree in writing, my area of greatest passion is for the worship arts. I am a choir director, playwright, songwriter, and choreographer. Outside of the worship arts, I am a business owner, professional speaker, trainer, publisher, newspaper columnist, and administrator. Because the worship arts market is still considered a "niche" or specialty demographic, I have been able to provide products for this market and outside of it.

Obey what the Lord tells you to do! Because I have a teaching gift, I offer classes through my online intensives. Through this model, I offer instruction in Book Writing and Publishing, Dance Company and Studio Management, Conference Planning and Event Management, and Kingdom Business. Our success stories abound! I am only able to do this as a result of having a track record of success in these areas. Again, do not imitate what you see someone else doing because it seems lucrative.

There are several marketplace ministers designing garments for ministry. I am excited to see creativity and diversity of design increasing in this area. Although many female dancers love flowing, beautiful garments, the Message that we deliver does not always mandate this presentation. Anyone who understands the fashion industry knows that it is nearly impossible to patent or trademark a garment design. Although many dance garment styles may look similar, those who are designing garments should never blatantly "knock off" the designs of a fellow minister. If you love the garments that you see created by someone else, support that ministry by purchasing them.

In many instances, those who sew garments also provide flags, banners, and glorious instruments of praise. Pageantry is a beautiful way to demonstrate the glory of God on earth. Flags can function in many shapes, sizes, and colors. Banners can range from the simple to the very ornate. Billows of various lengths and designs are being used more than ever before. Crowns, thrones, scepters, pillows, arks, crosses, and other visual treasuries are being inspired through the Word and by the Holy Spirit. We do not have to feel that we are on our own in learning how to master these crafts. If you ask, you may be surprised at who is willing to mentor you in this area.

Beyond the garments, tools, and books, there are limitless offerings in the area of products. Anointing oils, bags, t-shirts, prayer shawls, shofars, shoes, accessories, jewelry, calendars, and so much more continue to appear at the tables and online for purchase. Let Him do a new thing in you!

Legacy-Building

It has been often repeated that there is no success without a successor! We must not ascribe to the belief that if we are unable to do it, that it will not get completed. We must be intentional about how we train those we lead to be able to function as leaders in their own right.

In our dance company, we have many levels of leadership. I serve as the Artistic Director. We also have a Technical Trainer, Choreography Coach, Financial Administrator, Keeper of the Wardrobe, and Chaplain. Each of these leaders is mandated to identify and train at least one other member of the Company as an apprentice in their respective areas. This leadership structure allows me to continue to travel nationally and internationally without compromising the ability of the Company to have rehearsals or dance at events in my absence. While half of our team was in South Africa, the other half was able to dance for a major conference in our city without lowering the standard or damaging our reputation.

Identify the leadership structure within your organization. Is it working well? Are there areas that are currently lacking that need some additional attention or revision? Are you able to trust people to lead without micro-managing them? There is nothing wrong with altering something that is not working. If leaders continue to adopt a do-it-yourself mantra, we will be hindered from advancing further.

I also have an Executive Assistant to help me manage my growing responsibilities as a Director, mentor, wife and mother! Although I am blessed to wear many hats, I realized that I needed help to manage my growing collection. Help is not a dirty word!

You do not have to launch a formal mentoring program in order to pour into the life and ministry of someone else. Do not feel pressured to start a school, training program, or other organization just because people are willing to pay for instruction. Make sure that the legacy that you build is one that glorifies God and is one that He has uniquely appointed for you.

ADVANCING FURTHER

The Lord continues to open many doors for the advancement of dance ministry. One way that we are able to reach the world beyond physical travel is through media. Like anyone else, we must prepare for these opportunities and appearances so that we are able to represent the Gospel without compromise.

Wherever the industry sees an audience, there will be a platform provided. The film industry is no exception. Movement ministry has already appeared in a few independent films, and the exposure continues to develop. I believe that a day is coming when we will produce our own movies.

Television appearances are also becoming more widespread. Whether through interviews, special-interest stories, reality television, Gospel programming or scripted shows, praise dancers are leaping onto the small screen as well. I have been interviewed for television and online video uploads. After each appearance, I make sure to review the recording, and note any areas that I can improve for the future. When we utilize these doorways, we must remember that we are representing an entire populace of dancers and movement artists. What we do can open or close a door for someone else.

I have been interviewed at my local radio station and for internet radio on several occasions. As visual artists, we are unable to be seen over the airwaves, so we must also be able to paint a clear picture for our listeners. Know what you are talking about!

Take the initiative to get some very basic media training, at least. Record yourself speaking and listen. Are your thoughts and ideas expressed clearly? Do you listen before answering? What colors and hair-styles look best on you? Are you well-prepared?

If you hadn't noticed, the Christian and Gospel music industry is beginning to incorporate movement ministry during live appearances and also by including dance-centric songs on their projects. Dancers are being embraced on many levels. Although the "secular" industry has included dance production for decades, we are only now seeing this begin to expand for ministries.

I currently reside in Las Vegas, Nevada. For many tourists, this place symbolizes gambling and rampant sin. For me, it is a land of opportunity. Every month, God has opened a door for us to worship Him with passionate abandon on the famous Las Vegas Strip. We dance at the House of Blues Gospel Brunch inside the Mandalay Bay Hotel and Casino on a recurring basis. From the appearance of the venue, one would think that it would be difficult to represent the Lord there. I am a witness that there have been countless times that we have forgotten that we were dancing before an audience and had "church" right there on that stage! With the countless number of world-famous artists that have concerts on that stage, we are humbled that God would allow us to represent Him on the same platform, without having a "big name" ourselves.

In addition to weddings, family reunions, and large conferences, He has also granted us legendary stages on several occasions. We have been invited to minister for city-wide Gospel Fests, community celebrations, and ticketed events. Most recently, we were privileged to dance in a world-famous hotel and casino on the same stage that Elvis Presley performed for many years. All of this was able to be done without compromising the name of Jesus. Let God do it!

Las Vegas is embracing the arts in unprecedented ways. A multi-million dollar facility named "The Smith Center for Performing Arts" was built here for dance, music, and performing artists in a non-casino, family-friendly environment. It is state-of-the-art in every way imaginable.

Many of the libraries here also have stages that can be used for productions. Reign Dance Company was able to host our first dance production on a professional stage with lights, music, and a near-capacity crowd. Through this ticketed event, we were able to garner some much-needed financing for our Company.

I have twice been blessed to host praise dance concerts in public on the Las Vegas Strip. In full praise dance attire and with "Jesus music," we ministered to hundreds of people outdoors in the midst of drinking, smoking, and revelry. The big casinos and lights were in full view while we danced for His glory. Souls were won during these concerts. At the end of the last concert, I remember seeing a woman face-down on the concrete, in full view of onlookers, worshipping God. Any questions?

We are only limited by our own disobedience. Dance leaders who are ready to advance must be fully submitted to God so that we will not falter. Leading is a weighty responsibility that cannot be taken lightly. If we become selfish in our motives, it will only lead to our own demise. Our lives must be committed to prayer, diligent study, and healthy fellowship so that we can remain productive.

Dance leaders must advance, but we also need to help, love, edify and support each other to do this effectively. Is there a leader that models the type of ministry that inspires you? Reach out to them. Do you have a God-given dream or vision and have no idea where to begin? Connect with someone successful and glean from them. Are you feeling broken, tired, neglected, hindered, sabotaged, unsupported or abandoned? Run to God's presence right now and let Him heal you from the inside out. It is your moment for advancement. Seize it now!

REKESHA PITTMAN

Rekesha Pittman has been in training for ministry from her youth. Whether she is singing, dancing, acting, or speaking publicly, the Lord has graced her to be able to stand before His congregation with boldness. Her intense desire for ministerial excellence has opened the doors for her to minister in both dance and teaching of the Word on a National and International level.

Rekesha is a teacher of the Word and serves as workshop facilitator, mentor, consultant, and intercessor for various dance ministries, churches, worship arts departments, and music ministries. She is married to Matthew Pittman, a dynamic musician and ministry supporter and is the blessed mother of Lynynn Pittman. Her innermost desire is that pleasing the Lord be the focus of service in ministry, and that worship is an essential component in the daily life of every believer in the Body of Christ.

For booking, correspondence, or for additional information, please visit:

RekeshaPittman.com

REIGNAISSANCE PUBLICATIONS

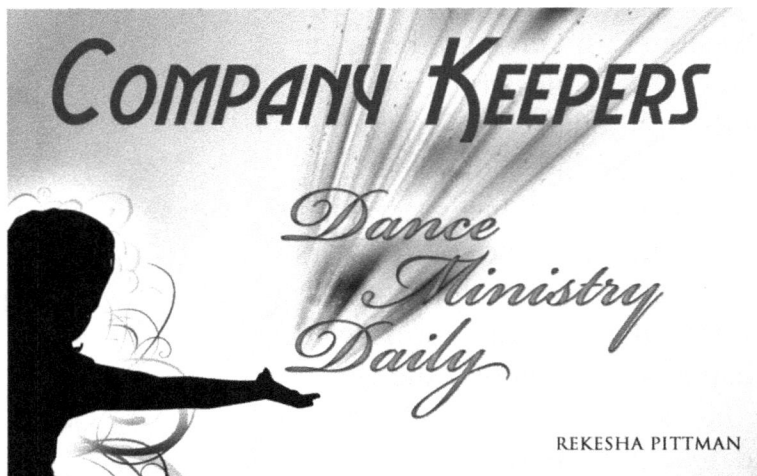

COMPANY KEEPERS

Dance Ministry Daily

REKESHA PITTMAN

Dance ministry preparation begins long before a song is selected. Daily study and insight will lead the dance minister into a more rewarding and impactful experience in the ministry of movement. Contained in these pages are revelation and application for the beginning dancer as well as the seasoned movement minister. Let these daily reminders serve as a testimony that we live, move, and have our being in Him as we move beyond the platform and exercise His Word in our hearts and spirits.

ORDER YOUR COPY TODAY!

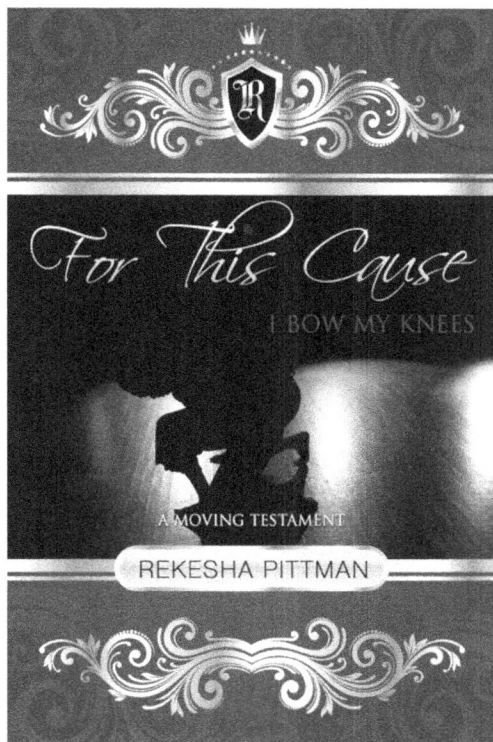

"For This Cause I Bow My Knees: A Moving Testament" will uplift, inspire, and inform the reader concerning the ministry of movement. Whether just starting a ministry or functioning as a seasoned veteran, this book will answer many questions or confirm what has already been revealed by the Spirit.

ORDER YOUR COPY TODAY!

DANCE MINISTRY MENTOR
with Rekesha Pittman!

Specialized Workshops
Group Coaching
Online Training Sessions
Ministry Retreats

www.DanceMinistryMentor.com